Notes Of Class Talks And Lectures-III

by

Swami Vivekananda

Notes Of Class Talks And Lectures-III
by Swami Vivekananda

ISBN: 978-93-59393-55-1

Published by

DOUBLE 9 BOOKS

2/13-B, Ansari Road
Daryaganj, New Delhi – 110002
info@double9books.com
www.double9books.com
Tel. 011-40042856

ABOUT THE AUTHOR

Swami Vivekananda was born Narendranath Datta in India on January 12, 1863. He died on July 4, 1902, and was the most important student of the Indian saint Ramakrishna. He was an important part of bringing Vedanta and Yoga to the West. He is also charged with making people more aware of other religions and making Hinduism a major world religion. Vivekananda had a lot of success at the Parliament. In the years that followed, he gave hundreds of lectures across the United States, England, and Europe to spread the main ideas of Hinduism. He also started the Vedanta Society of New York and the Vedanta Society of San Francisco, which is now the Vedanta Society of Northern California. Both of these groups became the basis for Vedanta Societies in the West. Vivekananda was one of the most important philosophers and social reformers in India at the time. He was also one of the most successful and powerful Vedanta missionaries in the West.People now think of him as one of the most important people in modern India and Hinduism. Mahatma Gandhi said that after reading Vivekananda's works, he loved his country a thousand times more.

CONTENTS

On Art

In art, interest must be centred on the principal theme. Drama is the most difficult of all arts. In it two things are to be satisfied — first, the ears, and second, the eyes. To paint a scene, if one thing be painted, it is easy enough; but to paint different things and yet to keep up the central interest is very difficult. Another difficult thing is stage-management, that is, combining different things in such a manner as to keep the central interest intact.

On Music

There is science in Dhrupad, Kheyal, etc., but it is in Kirtana, i.e. in Mâthura and Viraha and other like compositions that there is real music — for there is feeling. Feeling is the soul, the secret of everything. There is more music in common people's songs, and they should be collected together. The science of Dhrupad etc., applied to the music of Kirtana will produce the perfect music.

On Mantra And Mantra-Chaitanya

The Mantra-Shâstris (upholders of the Mantra theory) believe that some words have been handed down through a succession of teachers and disciples, and the mere utterance of them will lead to some form of realisation. There are two different meanings of the word Mantra-chaitanya. According to some, if you practise the repetition of a certain Mantra, you will see the Ishta-Devatâ who is the object or deity of that Mantra. But according to others, the word means that if you practise the repetition of a certain Mantra received from a Guru not competent, you will have to perform certain ceremonials by which that Mantra will become Chetana or living, and then its repetition will be successful. Different Mantras, when they are thus "living", show different signs, but the general sign is that one will be able to repeat it for a long time without feeling any strain and that his mind will very soon be concentrated. This is about the Tantrika Mantras.

From the time of the Vedas, two different opinions have been held about Mantras. Yâska and others say that the Vedas have meanings, but the ancient Mantra-shastris say that they have no meaning, and that their use consists only in uttering them in connection with certain sacrifices, when they will surely produce effect in the form of various material enjoyments or spiritual knowledge. The latter arises from the utterance of the Upanishads.

On Conceptions Of Godhead

Man's inner hankering is to find some one who is free, that is, beyond the laws of nature. The Vedantins believe in such an Eternal Ishvara, while the Buddhists and the Sânkhyas believe only a Janyeshvara (created God), that is, a God who was a man before, but has become God through spiritual practice. The Purânas reconcile these two positions by the doctrine of Incarnation. That is, they say that the Janyeshvara is nothing but the Nitya (Eternal) Ishvara, taking by Mâyâ the form of a Janyeshvara. The argument of the Sankhyas against the doctrine of Eternal Ishvara, viz "how a liberated soul can create the universe", is based on false grounds. For you cannot dictate anything to a liberated soul. He is free, that is, he may do whatever he likes. According to the Vedanta, the Janyeshvaras cannot create, preserve, or destroy the universe.

On Food

You preach to others to be men but cannot give them good food. I have been thinking over this problem for the last four years. I wish to make an experiment whether something of the nature of flattened rice can be made out of wheat. Then we can get a different food every day. About drinking water, I searched for a filter which would suit our country. I found one pan-like porcelain vessel through which water was made to pass, and all the bacilli remained in the porcelain pan. But gradually that filter would itself become the hotbed of all germs. This is the danger of all filters. After continued searching I found one method by which water was distilled and then oxygen was passed into it. After this the water became so pure that great improvement of health was sure to result from its use.

On Sannyâsa And Family Life

Talking of the respective duties of a monk and a householder, Swamiji said:

A Sannyasin should avoid the food, bedding, etc., which have been touched or used by householders, in order to *save himself* — not from hatred towards them — so long as he has not risen to the highest grade, that is, become a Paramahamsa. A householder should salute him with "Namo Nârâyanâya", and a Sannyasin should bless the former.

मेरुसर्षपयोर्यद्वत् सूर्यखद्योतयोरिव ।
सरित्सागरयोर्यद्वत् तथा भिक्षुगृहस्थयो: ॥

— Like the difference between the biggest mountain and a mustard-seed, between the sun and a glow-worm, between the ocean and a streamlet, is the wide gulf between a Sannyasin and a householder.

Swami Vivekananda made everyone utter this and, chanting some Vedanta stanzas, said, "You should always repeat to yourselves these Shlokas. 'Shravana' not only means hearing from the Guru, but also repetition to our own selves. '

आवृत्तिरसकृदुपदेशात्

— Scriptural truth should be often repeated for such has been repeatedly enjoined' — In this Sutra of Vedanta, Vyasa lays stress on repetition."

On Questioning The Competency Of The Guru

In the course of a conversation Swamiji spiritedly remarked, "Leave off your commercial calculating ideas. If you can get rid of your attachment to a single thing, you are on the way to liberation. Do not see a public woman, or sinner, or Sâdhu. That vile woman also is the Divine Mother. A Sannyâsin says once, twice, that she is Mother; then he gets deluded again and says, 'Hence, O vile, unchaste woman!' At a moment all your ignorance may vanish. It is foolish talk that ignorance disperses gradually. There are disciples who have been devoted to the Guru even when he has fallen from the ideal. I have seen in Rajputana one whose spiritual teacher had turned a Christian, but who nevertheless went on giving him his regular dues. Give up your Western ideas. Once you have pledged your faith to a particular teacher, stick to him with all force. It is children who say that there is no morality in the Vedanta. Yes, they are right. Vedanta is above morality. Talk of high things, as you have become Sannyasins."

Shri Ramakrishna: The Significance Of His Life And Teachings

In a narrow society there is depth and intensity of spirituality. The narrow stream is very rapid. In a catholic society, along with the breadth of vision we find a proportionate loss in depth and intensity. But the life of Sri Ramakrishna upsets all records of history. It is a remarkable phenomenon that in Sri Ramakrishna there has been an assemblage of ideas deeper than the sea and vaster than the skies.

We must interpret the Vedas in the light of the experience of Sri Ramakrishna. Shankaracharya and all other commentators made the tremendous mistake to think that the whole of the Vedas spoke the same truth. Therefore they were guilty of torturing those of the apparently conflicting Vedic texts which go against their own doctrines, into the meaning of their particular schools. As, in the olden times, it was the Lord alone, the deliverer of the *Gita*, who partially harmonised these apparently conflicting statements, so with a view to completely settling this dispute, immensely magnified in the process of time, He Himself has come as Sri Ramakrishna. Therefore no one can truly understand the Vedas and Vedanta, unless one studies them in the light of the utterance of Sri Ramakrishna who first exemplified in his life and taught that these scriptural statements which appear to the cursory view as contradictory, are meant for different grades of aspirants and are arranged in the order of evolution. The whole world will undoubtedly forget its fights and disputes and be united in a fraternal tie in religious and other matters as a consequence of these teachings.

If there is anything which Sri Ramakrishna has urged us to give up as carefully as lust and wealth, it is the limiting of the infinitude of God by circumscribing it within narrow bounds. Whoever, therefore, will try to limit the infinite ideals of Sri Ramakrishna in that way, will go against him and be his enemy.

One of his own utterances is that those who have seen the chameleon only once, know only one colour of the animal, but those who have lived under the tree, know all the colours that it puts on. For this reason, no saying of Sri Ramakrishna can be accepted as authentic, unless it is verified by those who constantly lived with him and whom he brought up to fulfil his life's mission.

Such a unique personality, such a synthesis of the utmost of Jnana, Yoga, Bhakti and Karma, has never before appeared among mankind. The life of Sri Ramakrishna proves that the greatest breadth, the highest catholicity and the utmost intensity can exist side by side in the same individual, and that society also can be constructed like that, for society is nothing but an aggregate of individuals.

He is the true disciple and follower of Sri Ramakrishna, whose character is perfect and all-sided like this. The formation of such a perfect character is the ideal of this age, and everyone should strive for that alone.

On Shri Ramakrishna And His Views

By force, think of one thing at least as Brahman. Of course it is easier to think of Ramakrishna as God, but the danger is that we cannot form Ishvara-buddhi (vision of Divinity) in others. God is eternal, without any form, omnipresent. To think of Him as possessing any form is blasphemy. But the secret of image-worship is that you are trying to develop your vision of Divinity in one thing.

Shri Ramakrishna used to consider himself as an Incarnation in the ordinary sense of the term, though I could not understand it. I used to say that he was Brahman in the Vedantic sense; but just before his passing away, when he was suffering from the characteristic difficulty in breathing, he said to me as I was cogitating in my mind whether he could even in that pain say that he was an Incarnation, "He who was Râma and Krishna has now actually become Ramakrishna — but not in your Vedantic sense!" He used to love me intensely, which made many quite jealous of me. He knew one's character by sight, and never changed his opinion. He could perceive, as it were, supersensual things, while we try to know one's character by reason, with the result that our judgments are often fallacious. He called some persons his Antarangas or 'belonging to the inner circle', and he used to teach them the secrets of his own nature and those of Yoga. To the outsiders or Bahirangas he taught those parables now known as "Sayings". He used to prepare those young men (the former class) for his work, and though many complained to him about them, he paid no heed. I may have perhaps a better opinion of a Bahiranga than an Antaranga through his actions, but I have a superstitious regard for the latter. "Love me, love my dog", as they say. I love that Brahmin priest intensely, and therefore, love whatever he used to love, whatever he used to regard! He was afraid about me that I might create a sect, if left to myself.

He used to say to some, "You will not attain spirituality in this life." He sensed everything, and this will explain his apparent partiality to some. He, as a scientist, used to see that different people required different treatment.

None except those of the "inner circle" were allowed to sleep in his room. It is not true that those who have not seen him will not attain salvation; neither is it true that a man who has seen him thrice will attain Mukti (liberation).

Devotion as taught by Nârada, he used to preach to the masses, those who were incapable of any higher training.

He used generally to teach dualism. As a rule, he never taught Advaitism. But he taught it to me. I had been a dualist before.

Shri Ramakrishna: The Nation's Ideal

In order that a nation may rise, it must have a high ideal. Now, that ideal is, of course, the abstract Brahman. But as you all cannot be inspired by an abstract ideal, you must have a personal ideal. You have got that, in the person of Shri Ramakrishna. The reason why other personages cannot be our ideal now is, that their days are gone; and in order that Vedanta may come to everyone, there must be a person who is in sympathy with the present generation. This is fulfilled in Shri Ramakrishna. So now you should place him before everyone. Whether one accepts him as a Sâdhu or an Avatâra does not matter.

He said he would come once more with us. Then, I think, he will embrace Videha-Mukti (Absolute Emancipation). If you wish to work, you must have such an Ishta-Devatâ, or Guardian Angel, as the Christian nations call it. I sometimes imagine that different nations have different Ishta-Devatas, and these are each trying for supremacy. Sometimes I fancy, such an Ishta-Devata becomes powerless to do service to a nation.

Mercinaries In Religion

(Delivered in Minneapolis on November 26, 1893:
Reported in the Minneapolis Journal)

The Unitarian church was crowded yesterday morning by an audience anxious to learn something of eastern religious thought as outlined by Swami Vivekananda, a Brahmin priest, who was prominent in the Parliament of Religions at Chicago last summer. The distinguished representative of the Brahmin faith was brought to Minneapolis by the Peripatetic Club, and he addressed that body last Friday evening. He was induced to remain until this week, in order that he might deliver the address yesterday. . . .

Dr. H.M. Simmons, the pastor, . . . read from Paul's lesson of faith, hope and charity, and "the greatest of these is charity", supplementing that reading by a selection from the Brahmin scripture which teaches the same lesson, and also a selection from the Moslem faith, and poems from the Hindu literature, all of which are in harmony with Paul's utterances.

After a second hymn Swami Vivekandi [*sic*] was introduced. He stepped to the edge of the platform and at once had his audience interested by the recital of a Hindu story. He said in excellent English:

"I will tell you a story of five blind men. There was a procession in a village in India, and all the people turned out to see the procession, and specially the gaily caparisoned elephant. The people were delighted, and as the five blind men could not see, they determined to touch the elephant that they might acquaint themselves with its form. They were given the privilege, and after the procession had passed, they returned home together with the people, and they began to talk about the elephant. 'It was just like a wall,' said one. 'No it wasn't,' said another, 'it was like a piece of rope.' 'You are mistaken,' said a third, 'I felt him and it was just a serpent.' The discussion grew excited, and the fourth declared the elephant was like a pillow. The argument soon broke into more angry expressions, and the five blind men took to fighting. Along came a man with two eyes, and he said, 'My friends, what is the matter?' The disputation was explained, whereupon the new-comer said, 'Men, you are all right: the trouble is you touched the elephant at different points. The wall was the side, the rope was the tail, the serpent was the trunk, and the toes were the pillow. Stop your quarrelling;

you are all right, only you have been viewing the elephant from different standpoints."

Religion, he said, had become involved in such a quarrel. The people of the West thought they had the only religion of God, and the people of the East held the same prejudice. Both were wrong; God was in every religion.

There were many bright criticisms on Western thought. The Christians were characterised as having a "shopkeeping religion". They were always begging of God — "O God, give me this and give me that; O God, do this and do that." The Hindu couldn't understand this. He thought it wrong to be begging of God. Instead of begging, the religious man should give. The Hindu believed in giving to God, to his fellows, instead of asking God to give to them. He had observed that the people of the West, very many of them, thought a great deal of God, so long as they got along all right, but when the reverse came, then God was forgotten: not so with the Hindu, who had come to look upon God as a being of love. The Hindu faith recognised the motherhood of God as well as the fatherhood, because the former was a better fulfilment of the idea of love. The Western Christian would work all the week for the dollar, and when he succeeded he would pray, "O God, we thank thee for giving us this benefit", and then he would put all the money into his pocket; the Hindu would make the money and then give it to God by helping the poor and the less fortunate. And so comparisons were made between the ideas of the West and the ideas of the East. In speaking of God, Vivekanandi said in substance: "You people of the West think you have God. What is it to have God? If you have Him, why is it that so much criminality exists, that nine out of ten people are hypocrites? Hypocrisy cannot exist where God is. You have your palaces for the worship of God, and you attend them in part for a time once a week, but how few go to worship God. It is the fashion in the West to attend church, and many of you attend for no other reason. Have you then, you people of the West, any right to lay exclusive claim to the possession of God?"

Here the speaker was interrupted by spontaneous applause. He proceeded: "We of the Hindu faith believe in worshipping God for love's sake, not for what He gives us, but because God is love, and no nation, no people, no religion has God until it is willing to worship Him for love's sake. You of the West are practical in business, practical in great inventions, but we of the East are practical in religion. You make commerce your business; we make religion our business. If you will come to India and talk with the workman in the field, you will find he has no opinion on politics. He knows nothing of politics. But you talk to him of religion, and the humblest knows about monotheism, deism, and all the isms of religion. You ask:

"'What government do you live under?' and he will reply: 'I don't know. I pay my taxes, and that's all I know about it.' I have talked with your labourers, your farmers, and I find that in politics they are all posted. They are either Democrat or Republican, and they know whether they prefer free silver or a gold standard. But you talk to them of religion; they are like the Indian farmer, they don't know, they attend such a church, but they don't know what it believes; they just pay their pew rent, and that's all they know about it — or God."

The superstitions of India were admitted, "but what nation doesn't have them?" he asked. In summing up, he held that the nations had been looking at God as a monopoly. All nations had God, and any impulse for good was God. The Western people, as well as the Eastern people, must learn to "want God", and this "want" was compared to the man under water, struggling for air; he wanted it, he couldn't live without it. When the people of the West "wanted" God in that manner, then they would be welcome in India, because the missionaries would then come to them with God, not with the idea that India knows not God, but with love in their hearts and not dogma.

The Destiny Of Man

(Delivered in Memphis on January 17, 1894:
Reported in Appeal-Avalanche)

The audience was moderately large, and was made up of the best literary and musical talent of the city, including some of the most distinguished members of the legal fraternity and financial institutions.

The speaker differs in one respect in particular from some American orators. He advances his ideas with as much deliberation as a professor of mathematics demonstrates an example in algebra to his students. Kananda (In those days Swamiji was generally referred to by American Press as Vive Kananda.) speaks with perfect faith in his own powers and ability to hold successfully his position against all argument. He advances no ideas, nor make assertions that he does not follow up to a logical conclusion. Much of his lecture is something on the order of Ingersoll's philosophy. He does not believe in future punishment nor in God as Christians believe in Him. He does not believe the mind is immortal, from the fact that it is dependent, and nothing can be immortal except it is independent of all things. He says: "God is not a king sitting away in one corner of the universe to deal out punishment or rewards according to a man's deeds here on earth, and the time will come when man will know the truth, and stand up and say, 'I am God,' am life of His life. Why teach that God is far away when our real nature, our immortal principle is God?

"Be not deluded by your religion teaching original sin, for the same religion teaches original purity. When Adam fell, he fell from purity. (Applause) Purity is our real nature, and to regain that is the object of all religion. All men are pure; all men are good. Some objections can be raised to them, and you ask why some men are brutes? That man you call a brute is like the diamond in the dirt and dust — brush the dust off and it is a diamond, just as pure as if the dust had never been on it, and we must admit that every soul is a big diamond.

"Nothing is baser than calling our brother a sinner. A lioness once fell upon a flock of sheep and killed a lamb. A sheep found a very young lion, and it followed her, and he gave it suck, and it grew up with the sheep and learned to eat grass like a sheep. One day an old lion saw the sheep lion and tried to get it away from the sheep, but it ran away as he approached.

The big lion waited till he caught the sheep lion alone, and he seized it and carried it to a clear pool of water and said, 'You are not a sheep, but a lion; look at your picture in the water.' The sheep lion, seeing its picture reflected from the water, said, 'I am a lion and not a sheep.' Let us not think we are sheep, but be lions, and don't bleat and eat grass like a sheep.

"For four months I have been in America. In Massachusetts I visited a reformatory prison. The jailor at that prison never knows for what crimes the prisoners are incarcerated. The mantle of charity is thrown around them. In another city there were three newspapers, edited by very learned men, trying to prove that severe punishment was a necessity, while one other paper contended that mercy was better than punishment. The editor of one paper proved by statistics that only fifty per cent of criminals who received severe punishment returned to honest lives, while ninety per cent of those who received light punishment returned to useful pursuits in life.

"Religion is not the outcome of the weakness of human nature; religion is not here because we fear a tyrant; religion is love, unfolding, expanding, growing. Take the watch — within the little case is machinery and a spring. The spring, when wound up, tries to regain its natural state. You are like the spring in the watch, and it is not necessary that all watches have the same kind of a spring, and it is not necessary that we all have the same religion. And why should we quarrel? If we all had the same ideas the world would be dead. External motion we call action; internal motion is human thought. The stone falls to the earth. You say it is caused by the law of gravitation. The horse draws the cart and God draws the horse. That is the law of motion. Whirlpools show the strength of the current; stop the current and stagnation ensues. Motion is life. We must have unity and variety. The rose would smell as sweet by any other name, and it does not matter what your religion is called.

"Six blind men lived in a village. They could not see the elephant, but they went out and felt of him. One put his hand on the elephant's tail, one of them on his side, one on his tongue [trunk], one on his ear. They began to describe the elephant. One said he was like a rope; one said he was like a great wall; one said he was like a boa constrictor, and another said he was like a fan. They finally came to blows and went to pummelling each other. A man who could see came along and inquired the trouble, and the blind men said they had seen the elephant and disagreed because one accused the other of lying. 'Well,' said the man, 'you have all lied; you are blind, and neither of you have seen it.' That is what is the matter with our religion. We let the blind see the elephant. (Applause).

"A monk of India said, 'I would believe you if you were to say that I could press the sands of the desert and get oil, or that I could pluck the tooth from the mouth of the crocodile without being bitten, but I cannot believe you when you say a bigot can be changed.' You ask why is there so much variance in religions? The answer is this: The little streams that ripple down a thousand mountain sides are destined to come at last to the mighty ocean. So with the different religions. They are destined at last to bring us to the bosom of God. For 1,900 years you have been trying to crush the Jews. Why could you not crush them? Echo answers: Ignorance and bigotry can never crush truth."

The speaker continued in this strain of reasoning for nearly two hours, and concluded by saying: "Let us help, and not destroy."

Reincarnation

(Delivered in Memphis on January 19, 1894:
Reported in Appeal-Avalanche)

Swami Vive Kananda, the beturbaned and yellow-robed monk, lectured again last night to a fair-sized and appreciative audience at the La Salette Academy on Third street.

The subject was "Transmigration of the Soul, or "metempsychosis". Possibly Vive Kananda never appeared to greater advantage than in this role, so to speak. Metempsychosis is one of the most widely-accepted beliefs among the Eastern races, and one that they are ever ready to defend, at home or abroad. As Kananda said:

"Many of you do not know that it is one of the oldest religious doctrines of all the old religions. It was known among the Pharisees, among the Jews, among the first fathers of the Christian Church, and was a common belief among the Arabs. And it lingers still with the Hindus and the Buddhists.

"This state of things went on until the days of science which is merely a contemplation of energies. Now, you Western people believe this doctrine to be subversive of morality. In order to have a full survey of the argument, its logical and metaphysical features, we will have to go over all the ground. All of us believe in a moral governor of this universe; yet nature reveals to us instead of justice, injustice. One man is born under the best of circumstances. Throughout his entire life circumstances come ready made to his hands — all conducive to happiness and a higher order of things. Another is born, and at every point his life is at variance with that of his neighbour. He dies in depravity, exiled from society. Why so much impartiality [partiality] in the distribution of happiness?

"The theory of metempsychosis reconciles this disharmonious chord in your common beliefs. Instead of making us immoral, this theory give us the idea of justice. Some of you say: 'It is God's will.' This is no answer. It is unscientific. Everything has a cause. The sole cause and whole theory of causation being left with God, makes Him a most immoral creature. But materialism is as much illogical as the other. So far as we go, perception [causation?] involves all things. Therefore, this doctrine of the transmigration of the soul is necessary on these grounds. Here we are all born. Is this the first creation? Is creation something coming out of nothing? Analysed completely, this sentence is nonsense. It is not creation, but manifestation.

"A something cannot be the effect of a cause that is not. If I put my finger in the fire, the burn is a simultaneous effect, and I know that the cause of the burn was the action of my placing my finger in contact with the fire. And as in the case of nature, there never was a time when nature did not exist, because the cause has always existed. But for argument['s] sake, admit that there was a time when there was no existence. Where was all this mass of matter? To create something new would be the introduction of so much more energy into the universe. This is impossible. Old things can be re-created, but there can be no addition to the universe.

"No mathematical demonstration could be made that would have this theory of metempsychosis. According to logic, hypothesis and theory must not be believed. But my contention is that no better hypothesis has been forwarded by the human intellect to explain the phenomena of life.

"I met with a peculiar incident while on a train leaving the city of Minneapolis. There was a cowboy on the train. He was a rough sort of a fellow and a Presbyterian of the blue nose type. He walked up and asked me where I was from. I told him India. 'What are you?' he said. 'Hindu', I replied. 'Then you must go to hell', he remarked. I told him of this theory, and after [my] explaining it, he said he had always believed in it because he said that one day when he was chopping a log, his little sister came out in her clothes and said that she used to be a man. That is why he believed in the transmigration of souls. The whole basis of the theory is this: If a man's actions be good, he must be a higher being, and vice versa.

"There is another beauty in this theory — the moral motor [motive] it supplies. What is done is done. It says, 'Ah, that it were done better.' Do not put your finger in the fire again. Every moment is a new chance."

Vive Kananda spoke in this strain for some time, and he was frequently applauded.

Swami Vive Kananda will lecture again this after moon at 4 o'clock at La Salette Academy on "The Manners and Customs of India."

Comparative Theology

(Delivered in Memphis on January 21, 1894:
Reported in Appeal-Avalanche)

"Comparative Theology" was the subject of a discourse last night by Swami Vive Kananda at the Young Men's Hebrew Association Hall. It was the blue-ribbon lecture of the series, and no doubt increased the general admiration the people of this city entertain for the learned gentleman.

Heretofore Vive Kananda has lectured for the benefit of one charity-worthy object or another, and it can be safely said that he has rendered them material aid. Last night, however, he lectured for his own benefit. The lecture was planned and sustained by Mr. Hu L. Brinkley, one of Vive Kananda's warmest friends and most ardent admirers. In the neighbourhood of two hundred gathered at the hall last night to hear the eminent Easterner for the last time in this city.

The first question the speaker asserted in connection with the subject was: "Can there be such a distinction between religions as their creeds would imply?"

He asserted that no differences existed now, and he retraced the line of progress made by all religions and brought it back to the present day. He showed that such variance of opinion must of necessity have existed with primitive man in regard to the idea of God, but that as the world advanced step by step in a moral and intellectual way, the distinctions became more and more indistinct, until finally it had faded away entirely, and now there was one all-prevalent doctrine — that of an absolute existence.

"No savage", said the speaker, "can be found who does not believe in some kind of a god."

"Modern science does not say whether it looks upon this as a revelation or not. Love among savage nations is not very strong. They live in terror. To their superstitious imaginations is pictured some malignant spirit, before the thought of which they quake in fear and terror. Whatever he likes he thinks will please the evil spirit. What will pacify him he thinks will appease the wrath of the spirit. To this end he labours even against his fellow-savage."

The speaker went on to show by historical facts that the savage man went from ancestral worship to the worship of elephants, and later to gods, such as the God of Thunder and Storms. Then the religion of the world was polytheism. "The beauty of the sunrise, the grandeur of the sunset, the mystifying appearance of the star-bedecked skies, and the weirdness of thunder and lightning impressed primitive man with a force that he could not explain, and suggested the idea of a higher and more powerful being controlling the infinities that flocked before his gaze," said Vive Kananda.

Then came another period — the period of monotheism. All the gods disappeared and blended into one, the God of Gods, the ruler of the universe. Then the speaker traced the Aryan race up to that period, where they said: "We live and move in God. He is motion." Then there came another period known to metaphysics as the "period of Pantheism". This race rejected Polytheism and Monotheism, and the idea that God was the universe, and said "the soul of my soul is the only true existence. My nature is my existence and will expand to me."

Vive Kananda then took up Buddhism. He said that they neither asserted nor denied the existence of a God. Buddha would simply say, when his counsel was sought: "You see misery. Then try to lessen it." To a Buddhist misery is ever present, and society measures the scope of his existence. Mohammedans, he said, believed in the Old Testament of the Hindu [Hebrew] and the New Testament of the Christian. They do not like the Christians, for they say they are heretics and teach man-worship. Mohammed ever forbade his followers having a picture of himself.

"The next question that arises," said he, "are these religions true or are some of them true and some of them false? They have all reached one conclusion, that of an absolute and infinite existence. Unity is the object of religion. The multiple of phenomena that is seen at every hand is only the infinite variety of unity. An analysis of religion shows that man does not travel from fallacy to truth, but from a lower truth to a higher truth.

"A man brings in a coat to a lot of people. Some say the coat does not fit them. Well, you get out; you can't have a coat. Ask one Christian minister what is the matter with all the other sects that are opposed to his doctrines and dogmas, and he will answer: 'Oh, they're not Christians.' But we have better instruction than these. Our own natures, love, and science — they teach us better. Like the eddies to a river, take them away and stagnation follows. Kill the difference in opinions, and it is the death of thought. Motion is necessity. Thought is the motion of the mind, and when that ceases death begins.

"If you put a simple molecule of air in the bottom of a glass of water it at once begins a struggle to join the infinite atmosphere above. So it is with the soul. It is struggling to regain its pure nature and to free itself from this material body. It wants to regain its own infinite expansion. This is everywhere the same. Among Christians, Buddhists, Mohammedans, agnostic, or priest, the soul is struggling. A river flows a thousand miles down the circuitous mountain side to where it joins the seas, and a man is standing there to tell it to go back and start anew and assume a more direct course! That man is a fool. You are a river that flows from the heights of Zion. I flow from the lofty peaks of the Himalayas. I don't say to you, go back and come down as I did, you're wrong. That is more wrong than foolish. Stick to your beliefs. The truth is never lost. Books may perish, nations may go down in a crash, but the truth is preserved and is taken up by some man and handed back to society, which proves a grand and continuous revelation of God."

Buddhism, The Religion Of The Light Of Asia

(Delivered in Detroit on March 19, 1894:
Reported in Detroit Tribune)

Vive Kananda lectured to an audience of about 150 [according to the *Journal*, 500] at the Auditorium last night upon "Buddhism, the Religion of the Light of Asia." Honourable Don M. Dickinson introduced him to the audience.

"Who shall say that this system of religion is divine and that doomed?" asked Mr. Dickinson in his introductory remarks. "Who shall draw the mystic line?"

Vive Kananda reviewed at length the early religions of India. He told of the great slaughter of animals on the altar of sacrifice; of Buddha's birth and life; of his puzzling questions to himself over the causes of creation and the reasons for existence; of the earnest struggle of Buddha to find the solution of creation and life; of the final result.

Buddha, he said, stood head and shoulders above all other men. He was one, he said, [of] whom his friends or enemies could never say that he drew a breath or ate a crumb of bread but for the good of all.

"He never preached transmigration of the soul," said Kananda, "except he believed one soul was to its successor like the wave of the ocean that grew and died away, leaving naught to the succeeding wave but its force. He never preached that there was a God, nor did he deny there was a God.

"'Why should we be good?' his disciples asked of him.

"'Because', he said, 'you inherited good. Let you in your turn leave some heritage of good to your successors. Let us all help the onward march of accumulated goodness, for goodness' sake.'

"He was the first prophet. He never abused any one or arrogated anything to himself. He believed in our working out our own salvation in religion.

"'I can't tell you,' he said, on his deathbed, 'nor any one. Depend not on any one. Work out your own religion [salvation].'

"He protested against the inequality of man and man, or of man and beast. All life was equal, he preached. He was the first man to uphold the doctrine of prohibition in liquors. 'Be good and do good', he said. 'If there is a God, you have Him by being good. If there is no God, being good is good. He is to be blamed for all he suffers. He is to be praised for all his good.'

"He was the first who brought the missionaries into existence. He came as a saviour to the downtrodden millions of India. They could not understand his philosophy, but they saw the man and his teachings, and they followed him."

In conclusion Kananda said that Buddhism was the foundation of the Christian religion; that the catholic church came from Buddhism.

The Science Of Yoga

(Fragmentary notes of a lecture recorded
by Ida Ansell and reprinted from *Vedanta
and the West*, July-August 1957.)

*(Delivered at Tucker Hall, Alameda,
California, on April 13, 1900)*

The old Sanskrit word Yoga is defined as [Chittavrittinirodha]. It means that Yoga is the science that teaches us to bring the Chitta under control from the state of change. The Chitta is the stuff from which our minds are made and which is being constantly churned into waves by external and internal influences. Yoga teaches us how to control the mind so that it is not thrown out of balance into wave forms. . . .

What does this mean? To the student of religion almost ninety-nine per cent of the books and thoughts of religion are mere speculations. One man thinks religion is this and another, that. If one man is more clever than the others, he overthrows their speculations and starts a new one. Men have been studying new religious systems for the last two thousand, four thousand, years — how long exactly nobody knows. . . . When they could not reason them out, they said, "Believe!" If they were powerful, they forced their beliefs. This is going on even now.

But there are a set of people who are not entirely satisfied with this sort of thing. "Is there no way out?" they ask. You do not speculate that way in physics, chemistry, and mathematics. Why cannot the science of religion be like any other science? They proposed this way: If such a thing as the soul of man really exists, if it is immortal, if God really exists as the ruler of this universe — He must be [known] here; and all that must be [realised] in [your own] consciousness.

The mind cannot be analysed by any external machine. Supposing you could look into my brain while I am thinking, you would only see certain molecules interchanged. You could not see thought, consciousness, ideas, images. You would simply see the mass of vibrations — chemical and physical changes. From this example we see that this sort of analysis would not do.

Is there any other method by which the mind can be analysed as mind? If there is, then the real science of religion is possible. The science of Raja-Yoga claims there is such a possibility. We can all attempt it and succeed to a certain degree. There is this great difficulty: In external sciences the object is [comparatively easy to observe]. The instruments of analysis are rigid; and both are external. But in the analysis of the mind the object and the instruments of analysis are the same thing. . . . The subject and the object become one. . . .

External analysis will go to the brain and find physical and chemical changes. It would never succeed [in answering the questions]: What is the consciousness? What is your imagination? Where does this vast mass of ideas you have come from, and where do they go? We cannot deny them. They are facts. I never saw my own brain. I have to take for granted I have one. But man can never deny his own conscious imagination. .

The great problem is ourselves. Am I the long chain I do not see — one piece following the other in rapid succession but quite unconnected? Am I such a state of consciousness [for ever in a flux]? Or am I something more than that — a substance, an entity, what we call the soul? In other words, has man a soul or not? Is he a bundle of states of consciousness without any connection, or is he a unified substance? That is the great controversy. If we are merely bundles of consciousness, . . . such a question as immortality would be merely delusion. . . . On the other hand, if there is something in me which is a unit, a substance, then of course I am immortal. The unit cannot be destroyed or broken into pieces. Only compounds can be broken up. . . .

All religions except Buddhism believe and struggle in some way or other to reach such a substance. Buddhism denies the substance and is quite satisfied with that. It says, this business about God, the soul, immortality, and all that — do not vex yourselves with such questions. But all the other religions of the world cling to this substance. They all believe that the soul is the substance in man in spite of all the changes, that God is the substance which is in the universe. They all believe in the immortality of the soul. These are speculations. Who is to decide the controversy between the Buddhists and the Christians? Christianity says there is a substance that will live for ever. The Christian says, "My Bible says so." The Buddhist says, "I do not believe in your book." . . .

The question is: Are we the substance [the soul] or this subtle matter, the changing, billowing mind? . . . Our minds are constantly changing. Where is the substance within? We do not find it. I am now this and now that. I will believe in the substance if for a moment you can stop these changes. . . .

Of course all the beliefs in God and heaven are little beliefs of organised religions. Any scientific religion never proposes such things.

Yoga is the science that teaches us to stop the Chitta [the mind-stuff] from getting into these changes. Suppose you succeed in leading the mind to a perfect state of Yoga. That moment you have solved the problem. You have known what you are. You have mastered all the changes. After that you may let the mind run about, but it is not the same mind any more. It is perfectly under your control. No more like wild horses that dash you down. . . . You have seen God. This is no longer a matter of speculation. There is no more Mr. So-and-So, . . . no more books or Vedas, or controversy of preachers, or anything. You have been yourself: I am the substance beyond all these changes. I am not the changes; if I were, I could not stop them. I can stop the changes, and therefore I can never be the changes. This is the proposition of the science of Yoga. . . .

We do not like these changes. We do not like changes at all. Every change is being forced upon us. . . . In our country bullocks carry a yoke on their shoulders [which is connected by a pole with an oil press]. From the yoke projects a piece of wood [to which is tied a bundle of grass] just far enough to tempt the bullock, but he cannot reach it. He wants to eat the grass and goes a little farther [thereby turning the oil press]. . . . We are like these bullocks, always trying to eat the grass and stretching our necks to reach it. We go round and round this way. Nobody likes these changes. Certainly not! . . . All these changes are forced upon us. . . . We cannot help it. Once we have put ourselves in the machine, we must go on and on. The moment we stop, there is greater evil than if we continued forward. . . .

Of course misery comes to us. It is all misery because it is all unwilling. It is all forced. Nature orders us and we obey, but there is not much love lost between us and nature. All our work is an attempt to escape nature. We say we are enjoying nature. If we analyse ourselves, we find that we are trying to escape everything and invent ways to enjoy this and that. . . . [Nature is] like the Frenchman who had invited an English friend and told him of his old wines in the cellar. He called for a bottle of old wine. It was so beautiful, and the light sparkled inside like a piece of gold. His butler poured out a glass, and the Englishman quietly drank it. The butler had brought in a bottle of castor oil! We are drinking castor oil all the time; we cannot help it. . . .

[People in general] . . . are so reduced to machinery they do not . . . even think. Just like cats, dogs and other animals, they are also driven with the whip by nature. They never disobey, never think of it. But even they have some experience of life. . . .

[Some, however,] begin to question: What is this? What are all these experiences for? What is the Self? Is there any escape? Any meaning to life?
. . .

The good will die. The wicked will die. Kings will die, and beggars will die. The great misery is death. . . .All the time we are trying to avoid it. And if we die in a comfortable religion, we think we will see Johns and Jacks afterwards and have a good time.

In your country they bring Johns and Jacks down to show you [in Seances]. I saw such people numbers of times and shook hands with them. Many of you may have seen them. They bang the piano and sing "Beulah Land": America is a vast land. My home is on the other side of the world. I do not know where Beulah Land is. You will not find it in any geography. See our good comfortable religion! The old, old moth-eaten belief!

Those people cannot think. What can be done for them? They have been eaten up by the world. There is nothing in them to think. Their bones have become hollow, their brains are like cheese. . . . I sympathise with them. Let them have their comfort! Some people are evidently very much comforted by seeing their ancestors from Beulah Land.

One of these mediums offered to bring my ancestors down to me. I said, "Stop there. Do anything you like, but if you bring my ancestors, I don't know if I can restrain myself." The medium was very kind and stopped.

In our country, when we begin to get worried by things, we pay something to the priests and make a bargain with God. . . . For the time being we feel comforted, otherwise we will not pay the priests. A little comfort comes, but [it turns] into reaction shortly. . . . So again misery comes. The same misery is here all the time. Your people in our country says, "If you believe in our doctrine you are safe." Our people among the lower classes believe in your doctrines. The only change is that they become beggars. . . . But is that religion? It is politics — not religion. You may call it religion, dragging the word religion down to that sense. But it is not spiritual.

Among thousands of men and women a few are inclined to something higher than this life. The others are like sheep. . . . Some among thousands try to understand things, to find a way out. The question is: Is there a way out? If there is a way out, it is in the soul and nowhere else. The ways out from other sources have been tried enough, and all [have been found wanting]. People do not find satisfaction. The very fact that those myriads of theories and sects exist show that people do not find satisfaction.

The science of Yoga proposes this, that the one way out is through ourselves. We have to individualise ourselves. If there is any truth, we can [realise it as our very essence]. . . . We will cease being driven about by nature from place to place. . . .

The phenomenal world is always changing: [to reach the Changeless] that is our goal. We want to be That, to realise that Absolute, the [changeless] Reality. What is preventing us from realising that Reality? It is the fact of creation. The creative mind is creating all the time and gets mixed up with its own creation. [But we must also remember that] it is creation that discovered God. It is creation that discovered the Absolute in every individual soul. . . .

Going back to our definition: Yoga is stopping the Chitta, the mind-stuff, from getting into these changes. When all this creation has been stopped — if it is possible to stop it — then we shall see for ourselves what we are in reality. . . . The Uncreated, the One that creates, manifests itself.

The methods of Yoga are various. Some of them are very difficult; it takes long training to succeed. Some are easy. Those who have the perseverance and strength to follow it through attain to great results. Those who do not may take a simpler method and get some benefit out of it.

As to the proper analysis of the mind, we see at once how difficult it is to grapple with the mind itself. We have become bodies. That we are souls we have forgotten entirely. When we think of ourselves, it is the body that comes into our imagination. We behave as bodies. We talk as bodies. We are all body. From this body we have to separate the soul. Therefore the training begins with the body itself, [until ultimately] the spirit manifests itself. . . . The central idea in all this training is to attain to that power of concentration, the power of meditation.